AF575332

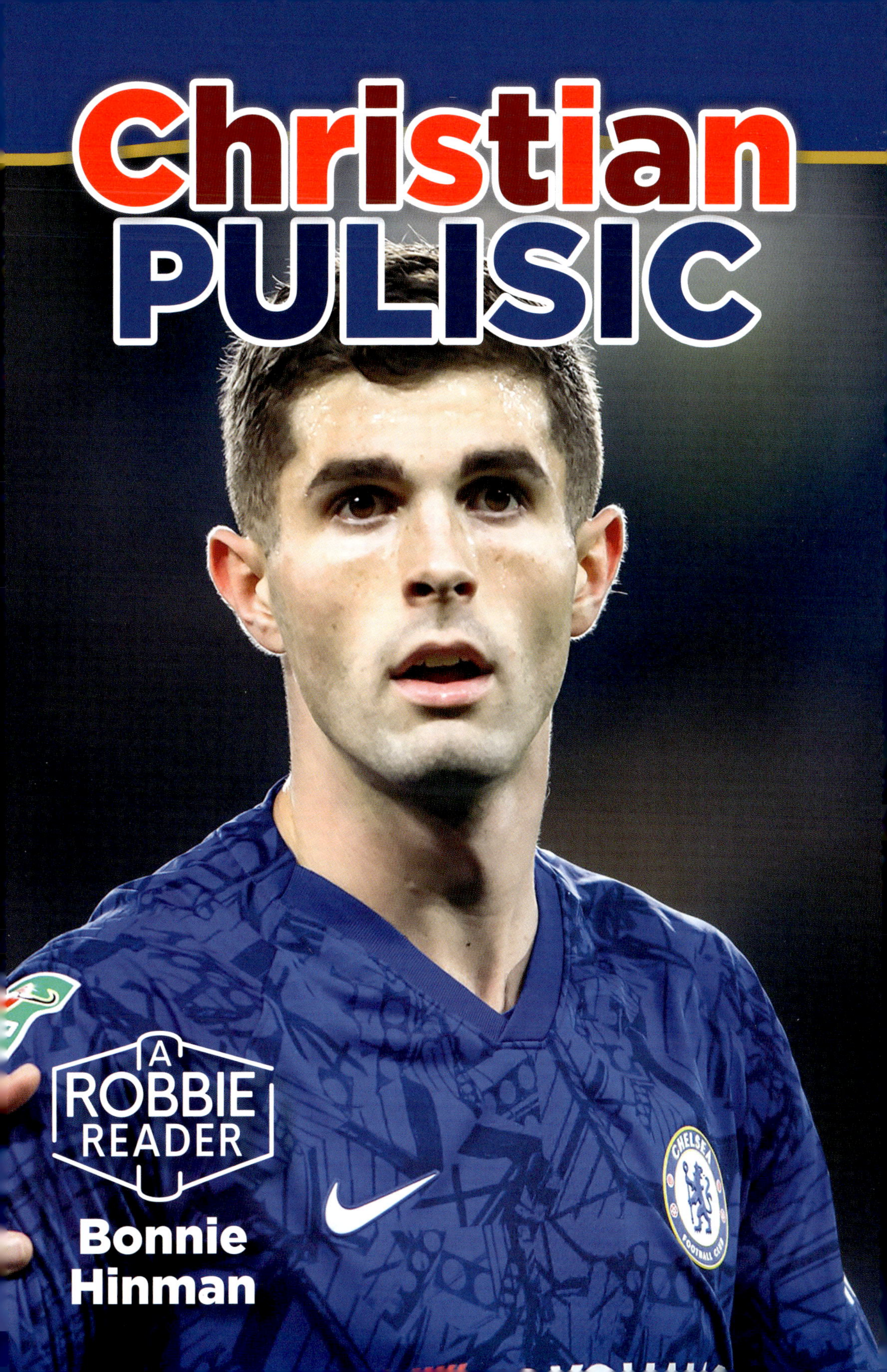
Christian
PULISIC
A
ROBBIE
READER
Bonnie
Hinman

2001 SW 31st Avenue
Hallandale, FL 33009

www.mitchelllane.com

First Edition, 2021.
Author: Bonnie Hinman
Designer: Ed Morgan
Editor: Morgan Brody

Series: Robbie Reader
Title: Christian Pulisic / by Bonnie Hinman

Hallandale, FL : Mitchell Lane Publishers, [2021]

Library bound ISBN: 978-1-58415-794-6
eBook ISBN: 978-1-58415-849-3

Little Mitchie is an imprint of Mitchell Lane Publishers.

PHOTO CREDITS: Design Elements, freepik.com, Cover: UK Sports Pics/SIPA/Newscom, p. 5 Tess Derry/ZUMA Press/Newscom, p. 7 John Walton/ZUMA Press/Newscom, p. 9 Shaun Brooks/Action Plus/Newscom, p. 11 Anthony Devlin/ZUMA Press/Newscom, p. 13 Guido Kirchner/dpa/picture-alliance/Newscom, p. 15 M.i.S./Pixathlon/SIPA/Newscom, p. 17 DYLAN MARTINEZ/REUTERS/Newscom, p. 19 Robin Alam/Icon Sportswire 164/Robin Alam/Icon Sportswire/Newscom, p. 20 John Todd/Isiphotos.Com/ZUMA Press/Newscom, p. 23 firo Sportphoto/ Christopher Neu/picture alliance / firo Sportpho/Newscom, pp. 24-25 Shaun Brooks/Action Plus/Newscom, p. 27 LEE SMITH/Action Images via Reuters/Newscom

Contents

Words in **bold** can be found in the Glossary.

CHAPTER **ONE**

Young Soccer Star

Christian Pulisic is the soccer star in the Pulisic family now. But it wasn't always that way. Christian started playing soccer in a youth league when he was only four years old. Christian's sister Dee Dee also played. She was a year and a half older than Christian. Pulisic's father coached both kids' teams.

Christian and Dee Dee's dad Mark says that Dee Dee was the soccer star back then. She'd get the ball and charge ahead. Christian was a lot less focused. Mark Pulisic said later of the young Christian. "He would look at people on the sidelines and wave at them as the game went on around him." Christian's parents cheered him on. They told him to just have fun.

Christian Pulisic's focus on the soccer pitch has helped him become a star player.

CHAPTER **ONE**

Christian Mate Pulisic was born on September 18, 1998, in Hershey, Pennsylvania. His parents, Mark and Kelley Pulisic both played soccer during college at George Mason University. Mark Pulisic played **professional** soccer briefly and coached as well.

By the time Christian was six, he found his focus. He played soccer without waving to bystanders during the games. When he was almost seven, his family moved to England. Christian's mom was a teacher. She received a **scholarship** to work on a teaching exchange program in England.

For a year the family lived in a small English village called Tackley. Christian joined a local soccer club, Brackley Town. "A lot of people don't realize but it really brought on my **passion** for the game." Pulisic said of his time playing soccer in England. "I just started to love it so much and I said: 'Wow. I'm pretty good! I think I can do something with this game.'" The seven-year-old seemed to have found his passion.

Pulisic plays winger for Chelsea FC.

CHAPTER **TWO**

Game Changer

While in England, Pulisic and his family traveled all over the country. Pulisic's dad said in an interview, "We were football crazy." The family went to professional soccer games in famous stadiums. Pulisic practiced and played soccer with friends. They didn't need a **scheduled** game. The back yard was fine for kicking around a soccer ball.

The Pulisic family returned to the U.S. in 2006. They moved to Michigan for a year before returning to Hershey, Pennsylvania. Pulisic played for the Michigan Rush during that year. Back in his hometown, Pulisic joined the PA Classics. It was a soccer **development** academy. He spent almost seven years with the PA Classics.

Pulisic's foot skills are one of his biggest advantages.

CHAPTER **TWO**

Pulisic's parents encouraged him to try other sports. He loved basketball. He often played **H-O-R-S-E** in the driveway with his dad. During this time Pulisic was limited to no more than four or five hours a week of organized soccer games and practices. His parents did not want him to burn out. However, he practiced endlessly whenever there was a ball within reach. He would get his mom or dad to come outside and stand in front of a small net. He fired shot after shot toward them.

During his years with PA Classics, Pulisic also spent time at camps and clinics. He trained with European clubs for short times. His family called these trips soccer vacations. These trips allowed soccer coaches to see what Christian could do. But they also helped him get used to new, uncomfortable situations. In those places he wasn't the best player in his group.

Game Changer

By age fourteen it was clear that Pulisic was headed toward an outstanding future in soccer. His parents believed that it was time for young Christian to train in Europe at one of the youth academies. That decision led to his move to Germany to train at the Borussia Dortmund Academy. This turned out to be a game-changer for Pulisic's soccer career.

Pulisic also plays for the USA National Team.

CHAPTER **THREE**

2016: The Breakout Year

Pulisic and his father moved to Germany in early 2015. Pulisic's grandfather, Mate was born in Croatia. This meant that Pulisic could claim **dual** citizenship. This fact allowed Pulisic to get an EU passport.

"As a result of my dual citizenship, I've been able to play in Europe, training at the Dortmund Academy, since I was 16," Pulisic explained in an interview. "Without it, I would have had to wait until I was 18. And for a soccer player, those years are everything." He went on to say, "From a developmental **perspective**, it's almost like this sweet spot, where a player's growth and skill sort of intersect, in just the right way—where a player can make their biggest leap in development by far."

In January 2016 Pulisic signed with the Borussia Dortmund professional team.

CHAPTER **THREE**

Pulisic made the most of the good luck given him by his grandfather. He moved steadily from one youth team to the next. In January 2016 he signed with Borussia Dortmand's professional team. This team was a member of the Bundesliga League. Soon Pulisic began breaking records. He became the youngest non-German player to score in the Bundesliga League. Shortly after, he became the youngest Bundesliga player ever to score two goals in a game.

Pulisic had played for the Under 17 and Under 19 U.S. National Teams. He was called up to the senior U.S. National Team in March 2016. Two days after being called up, Pulisic became the youngest American to play in a World Cup qualifier. In May he became the youngest player to score for the U.S. team in the modern era.

Pulisic was the youngest Bundesliga League player ever to score two goals in a game.

2016: The Breakout Year

The firsts continued to roll in. He was the youngest to score in a World Cup Qualification match for the U.S. And finally, he became the youngest American to start in a World Cup Qualifier match. The year 2016 was clearly Pulisic's breakout year.

CHAPTER **FOUR**

The Big Disappointment

Christian Pulisic plays as a mid-field attacker or winger. He can make and take passes in difficult positions on the **pitch**. He can dribble the ball fast. Pulisic can play equally well with either foot.

Pulisic uses a hard driving approach. He is not afraid to push the ball right up to opponents. He often gets shoved or even knocked down by the other team's players. This can lead to a penalty shot which gives Pulisic's team a chance to score.

Pulisic's style of play means he often gets fouled by other players.

CHAPTER **FOUR**

In Pulisic's first full season with Borussia Dortmund, he made 43 appearances. He scored five goals. He helped his team win the DFB Cup, which is a competition for the German Football Association. At that time he became the youngest American to win a major European trophy.

In international play, Pulisic was named U.S. Men's National Team Player of the Year in 2017. In nine appearances he scored six goals. This was during the final months for national teams to **qualify** for the 2018 World Cup. Held every four years, the 2018 contest was to be held in Russia. Pulisic did well for the U.S. team by scoring goals in qualifying games in the fall of 2017.

U.S. Men's National Team general manager Earnie Stewart poses with Pulisic after the young player was awarded the Best Young Player award in July 2019.

CHAPTER **FOUR**

Pulisic plays all out for the U.S. National Team in a 2018 FIFA World Cup Qualifier game against Trinidad and Tobago in October 2017.

The Big Disappointment

In spite of Pulisic's efforts, the U.S. Men's National Team still failed to qualify for the 2018 World Cup. It was a **bitter** loss for Pulisic and the other team members. It was the first time the U.S. team had failed to qualify for the World Cup since 1986.

The U.S. team played Trinidad and Tobago on October 10, 2017. The score was 1–2 with the U.S. trailing. Pulisic later wrote about that awful defeat. "We had to at least tie. Had to have that last goal. And we were grinding for it like crazy, right up to the very end. But we didn't get it. And once we didn't get it and were walking off that field—well, that's when I pretty much knew. I knew it was over."

CHAPTER **FIVE**

Back to England

Pulisic's 2017–2018 season with Borussia Dortmund was a solid one. He appeared 42 times in league and cup games. He scored five goals, the same as the 2016–2017 season. In December 2018 Pulisic took second place for the Kopa Trophy. Organized by *France Football*, the Kopa Trophy is awarded to the best performing soccer player under the age of 21.

Frustration with a referee's call shows during a Borussia Dortmund game in 2019.

Pulisic's 2018–2019 season was hard. He started fewer games for Borussia Dortmund with only 30 appearances. Even so he still scored more goals than in the previous season. Good season or not, Pulisic was offered a trade to Chelsea football club in England. Pulisic signed the deal on January 2, 2019. Chelsea paid Borussia Dortmund a $73 million transfer fee for Pulisic. It was the highest fee ever paid for an American. Chelsea immediately loaned Pulisic back to Borussia Dortmund for the rest of the season.

CHAPTER **FIVE**

The Chelsea football club is a member of the Premier League. The Premier League is one of the best in the world. Pulisic's move to Chelsea before he was 21 was a huge prize. Pulisic reported to training early in the summer. After that he played well in several non-league games called friendlies.

Chelsea's official season began in August. Pulisic came in as a **substitute** in a pre-season game on August 6, 2019. Chelsea manager Frank Lampard said of Pulisic's performance, "So I'm really happy with him and I think there's lots, lots more to come, all good signs again for what he can be to the club."

Back to England

Pulisic began his first season with the Chelsea football club in August 2019.

CHAPTER **FIVE**

On August 11, 2019, Pulisic played in his first official Premier League game as a substitute. His first start for Chelsea came on August 14. In an outstanding game on October 26, 2019, Pulisic scored his first goals for Chelsea. He scored three goals also known as a hat trick.

Christian Pulisic is racing toward an outstanding career in soccer. At 21 he's not so different than he was at age 7. He loves to play and he wants to win.

Christian Pulisic loves soccer and likes to celebrate a good game.

Timeline

1998 Christian is born on September 18, 1998, in Hershey, Pennsylvania.

2005 Lives in England for a year.

Plays for Brackley Town youth team.

2006 Returns to the United States to play for the Michigan Rush.

2007 Joins PA Classics Development Academy.

2015 Moves to Germany to train at Borussia Dortmund Academy.

Played with Under 17 and Under 19 youth teams.

2016 Signs with Borussia Dortmund professional team in January.

Called up to play with the U.S. National Team in March.

Became the youngest American to start in a World Cup Qualifier match.

Named U.S. Soccer's Young Male Player of the Year.

2017 Helps Borussia Dortmund win the DFB Cup.

Youngest American to win a major European trophy.

Named U.S. Men's National Team Player of the Year.

Plays with U.S. team when it failed to qualify for the 2018 World Cup.

2018 Takes second place for the Kopa Trophy.

2019 Transfers to Chelsea football club in England in January.

On loan to Borussia Dortmund for remainder of season.

Plays as substitute in first Premier League game for Chelsea on August 11.

Starts in first Premier League game on August 14.

Scores a hat trick for Chelsea on October 26.

Find Out More

Books

DK. *DK Eyewitness Books: Soccer*. New York: DK Publishing, 2018.

Jokulsson, Illugi. *Stars of All Time (World Soccer Legends)*. New York: Abbeville Press, 2017.

Latham, Andrew. *Soccer Smarts for Kids: 60 Skills, Strategies, and Secrets*. Emeryville, California: Rockridge Press, 2016.

Websites

Christian Pulisic's Facebook Page
https://www.facebook.com/cmpulisic/

Official website of the Premier League
https://www.premierleague.com/home

Official website of Chelsea Football Club
http://www.chelseafc.com/en

Works Consulted

Ames, Nick. "Christian Pulisic: The Making of a Young Man Ready to Step Up." *The Guardian*. May 31, 2016. https://www.theguardian.com/football/blog/2016/may/31/Christian-pulisic-usa-soccer-copa-america-2016

Bird, Liviu. "U.S. Prospect Christian Pulisic a Fast-Rising Talent at Borussia Dortmund." *Planet Futbol USA*. January 20, 2016. https://www.si.com/planet-futbol/2016/01/21/christian-pulisic-usa-borussia-dortmund

Bonn, Kyle. "Christian Pulisic Can Become Star at Chelsea." NBC Sports. August 5, 2019. https://soccer.nbcsports.com/2019/08/05/christian-pulisic-can-become-true-star-at-chelsea/

Borden, Sam. "Chelsea's Christian Pulisic is Not Your Wonderboy Anymore." ESPN. August 2, 2019. https://www.espn.com/soccer/story/3910275/chelseas-christian-pulisic-is-not-your-wonderboy-anymore

Works Consulted *continued*

Carlisle, Jeff. "U.S.'s Christian Pulisic 'Not Going to Change' Style in Face of Multiple Fouls." ESPN. October 5, 2017. https://www.espn.com/soccer/united-states/story/3221168/uss-christian-pulisic-not-going-to-change-style-in-face-of-multiple-fouls

Dohrmann, George. "The Christian Pulisic Blueprint." *Bleacher Report*. June 7, 2017. https://bleacherreport.com/articles/2713937-the-christian-pulisic-blueprint

McIntyre, Doug. "Premier League Preview: Why Christian Pulisic Can Become an Instant Chelsea Star." Yahoo Sports. August 5, 2019. https://sports.yahoo.com/premier-league-preview-why-christian-pulisic-can-become-an-instant-chelsea-star-143503313.html

Metro Sport Reporter. "Frank Lampard Says There is 'More to Come' From Christian Pulisic After Full Chelsea Debut in Super Cup." *Metro*. August 15, 2019. https://metro.co.uk/2019/08/15/frank-lampard-christian-pulisic-chelsea-debut-performance-liverpool-10574962/

Mitten, Andy. "Why Christian Pulisic is One of Football's Most Exciting Young Talents." *GQ Magazine-Britain*. January 2, 2019. https://www.gq-magazine.co.uk/article/christian-pulisic-is-footballs-most-exciting-young-talent

Pitzer, Kurt. "Meet Christian Pulisic, the U.S. Soccer Team's 17-Year-Old Wunderkind to Watch as Copa America Kicks Off." *People*. June 3, 2016. https://people.com/sports/meet-christian-pulisic-the-u-s-soccer-teams-youngest-player/

Pulisic, Christian. "1,834 Days." *The Players Tribune*. November 13, 2017. https://www.theplayerstribune.com/en-us/articles/christian-pulisic-usmnt-world-cup

Smith, Andy. "How Did Borussia Dortmund Star Christian Pulisic Make It Into the European Big Leagues?" *Bundesliga*. 2018. https://www.bundesliga.com/en/news/Bundesliga/how-did-christian-pulisic-make-it-into-the-european-big-leagues-dortmund-512258.jsp

Glossary

bitter
Disagreeable or painful

development academy
A school that educates and improves an athlete's skills

dual
Having two kinds or parts

H-O-R-S-E
A basketball game often played with just a ball and a hoop

passion
A great love or interest in something

perspective
A particular way of looking or understanding something

pitch
A soccer playing field

professional
Playing a sport or doing something for money to make a living

qualify
To meet requirements to advance in a series of games or other contests

scheduled
To do something at a time decided upon earlier

scholarship
Money or aid given to help a student pay for school

substitute
Playing a game or other activity in the place of another

Index

About the **Author**

Bonnie Hinman has written more than 60 books for young people. Many were biographies. Christian Pulisic has lived an amazing life for someone so young. Hinman admires that his family has provided him with such a down-to-earth childhood and supports him in all that he does. Hinman lives in Southwest Missouri with her husband Bill near her children and grandchildren.